Probably
Inevitable

Matthew Tierney

Coach House Books, Toronto

first edition

 Canada Council   Conseil des Arts    ONTARIO ARTS COUNCIL   Canadä
for the Arts   du Canada   CONSEIL DES ARTS DE L'ONTARIO

Published with the generous assistance of the Canada Council for the Arts
and the Ontario Arts Council. Coach House Books also acknowledges the
support of the Government of Canada through the Canada Book Fund and
the Government of Ontario through the Ontario Book Publishing Tax Credit.

LIBRARY AND ARCHIVES CANADA CATALOGUING IN PUBLICATION

Tierney, Matthew Frederick, 1970-
      Probably inevitable / Matthew Tierney.

Poems.
Issued also in an electronic format.
ISBN 978-1-55245-261-5

      I. Title.

PS8589.I42P76 2012   C811'.6   C2012-904673-6

Probably Inevitable is available as an ebook: ISBN 978 1 77056 318 6.

Purchase of the print version of this book entitles you to a free digital copy.
To claim your ebook of this title, please email sales@chbooks.com with
proof of purchase or visit chbooks.com/digital. (Coach House Books reserves
the right to terminate the free digital download offer at any time.)

For my brothers,
Geoffrey, Aaron, Peter & Luke

Contents

All of the heroes
you see falling down
were filmed trying to stand
up.
                    – Mary Ruefle

Author's
Note to Self

They keep reminding me you're without foghorn. Unlikely
this missive will end before you've determined it's possible
to navigate by hi-hat alone. Bad idea. Cymbals aren't usually

cymbals, they're mermaids. Inland we've taken to mounting
birth certificates to establish the thickness of drywall. Thus far
mine (ours) hangs askew from last month's tremors, nothing

a dog lick couldn't set straight. While boiling broth today I heard
eighth notes mingle in a downstream draft. Thought to myself:
all art aspires to the well-crafted pop song. Then a supernova

went off and optical fibres bobbed like anemones in the deep.
It's been one petit mal after another. But enough about me.
How're those chilblains? Tolerable? My support group says

ailments I've blamed on you are narrative issues in spite of
the unforgiving arctic wind. You're captain, you've shouldered
a yeoman's share, I should cut you some slack re: the untimely

loss of my cockatiel. Steadfast above the long-range forecast,
its pitch-perfect imitation of our doorbell's reveille never failed
to move me. Now I'm hours on the ottoman staring at its cage

until an intestinal jab sends me to the low-flush. So depressing,
waiting to rehit the button like some percussionist. You'll be
happy to learn I've cut out the supplements, though (my mistake)

I bought in bulk a year's worth of birdseed. My nutritionist,
she's high on ancient whole grains, I can never stock enough
tobacco tins of quinoa or spelt, so naturally it got me thinking –

Okay, that part's made up. Never allowed a pet, was I? Please,
no sugar-coating, explain what you meant by *Incompatible*
with your peccadilloes. I admit only a weakness for pink noise

and a modest collection of boosted artwork. This tristesse,
black bile, what you under Munch-red sky write off as o-c,
it's my strategy for keeping time. Mostly I can't get over how

the toilet's gargle sounds like a hectic call centre. You're tacking
along Big Sur or Ha Long or Hadselfjorden, your head turns,
wake feathers past the bow, you're not sure … yes, an echo off

porcelain tiles. Suddenly I've lost count: how many honks make
a metaphor? Don't answer that. I wouldn't want you abstracted.
It's me who finds the Sleuth of Baker Street a bore, the dean

more fortune's fool than clown. Joint rasp, lid spasm: also me.
Sun in sync with a sawtooth vee (where does this come from?)
like a rusty chest retractor, you squint against snowcap glare

as regrets grow melodious, take a hard look at the lead goose …
Right. Enough about me. You can see the cheque's made out
to CASH. After much internal debate, I left the memo line blank.

One

Speed Dating
in the Milky Way

My lower limbs
on the Schwinn Elliptical
trace ovals in Euclidean space, 7 min, 12 sec
since I laced up, applied digital pressure
to QUICK START my regimen. Ten of us
pseudo-running towards ten identical moues
afloat storeys high in Bally's street-facing windows.
Grim, bluecoat infantrymen
certain a jammed flintlock plays in their future.
We choose flight over fight, study our dashboards,
the kilometres' uptick, calories' red shift.
First law of thermodynamics holds
like a well-pitched pup tent in a rainstorm;
change in my internal E
fogging concave lenses, myopia itself evidence
of a tipsy work/life balance. Much as I try to feign
zero interest in your metabolism,
i.e., whether it might be free later
for a gourmet burger and low-watt rom-com,
it's too easy to check out your reflection
not to. Could this be
what Einstein was thinking
when he lit on his special theory? Our ability
to fixate on the adjunct or disagreement
at the expense of eye to eye. If you and I happily ever
pass each other on the street
in the faraway once-upon, we might find grounds
for a meaningful relationship. We would, however,
quibble over the movie's start time

in a theatre near Andromeda.
Should the moment arrive, threaten to derail
our genetic mandate, I'm here to tell you
we'd both be right. Honey,
it breaks us, but there's no absolute.
Time's not the market, it's the bustle;
not the price, but worth.
The haggle, sleight, flirt. *Hello*,
was that a look? Or euphoria sweetening the pot?
Mean solar age and gravitational weight
say I've sustained my heart's optimum rate
across the eight-minute tickertape – roughly when
this twilight departed the sun.
All we share are endorphins
and a longing to twin circadian rhythms
with that special someone on a plush California king
about to go superluminal. My/your
sweatdrops bounce off the gym floor
like hot shells during a massacre,
evaporate into chalk outlines
of giant amoebas
circumscribed by the circles we define as coincident.

Rising Action,
Then Falling

Every make and model, it seems,
scrolls past like begats in the King James.
The word *yield*, face out inside its equilateral
yellow field, makes a case for progress as noun
and whim. My left turn signal counters
with notions of a clockwork universe,
my stomach walls continue to spaghettify.
All intelligent species need increasingly
richer resources: hotels on Marvin Gardens, high-
energy plankton, artesian wells. *The Wind-Up*
Bird Chronicle has entire chapters set at the bottom
of a black hole, Murakami's protagonist in deep
(as usual) with cats and existential shadows.
He's moved more copies than a cancer cell.
Late summer memories bead like humidity
on window-mounted air conditioners,
I believe approaching heat stroke or heat death
could rob me of my chance to upgrade
the more fragile human parts: titanium hips
and a cloned pig's heart, so I can outlive my shame
at underachieving on the LSAT. I've since learned
pusillanimity rarely gets you noticed –
goddamn, people, this off-ramp ain't no rooftop
helipad. We think little of what we're doing
while we're doing, which tells us we think
too much. Expansion brings diminishing returns;
Freeman Dyson figured an evolved 'we' could nest
in a white dwarf, ratchet down our metabolism,
dispense a single thought every millennium.

I really hope not to have 20,000 years of
'C'mon buddy, let me in.' Anxiety
is what happens if nothing else does,
I'm late for my appointed genre (dramedy),
a decade since my last metaphysical.
Parse a finite interval infinitely and you're
Bill Murray in *Groundhog Day* or Georg Cantor
or both, hallucinogen making lucid
the dog-and-pony show of fine motor control.
Some engines power down when idling,
it's ingenious how people put their heads together
and come up with reactions that make sense.
Raindrops fall like opportunities from past lives,
two-to-one I'm wasting something besides
the morning. The bird I remember
on a branch outside the kitchen window
just sounded like it was being wound up,
a jack-in-a-box ignoring the weasel pop.
Vehicles outfox my reflexes like fusion jazz,
a Corolla rolls into view, the driver
with million-mile stare just another closet novelist
who'd gladly sacrifice character for plot.
Give her half a chance and a heartbeat.

Seldom Rarely Never

When she wakes
she wakes having dreamt
she's had a bad sleep.
East-lit window ajar,
bushes bright as ash,
beds of jostling swans.
Once lucid, she's sure
some expected thing
will drop to the lawn,
she's not sure what.
Above all, stay positive.
The mirror looks on her
not unkindly, hums a
newly familiar tune.
Clothed, she descends
and enters the kitchen
and the hardwood creaks
as if her dance card's full.
Is it unreal or surreal?
What's the proper term
for feeling so normal?
She stands sipping tea
while sprites complete
routine figure eights.
Such unwonted grace
in the Virginia creeper,
enough not to notice
privacy screen or fence.

V Is for Vacuum

On the flip side
he's in sweatpants moving house,
groping for a contact lens
in the carpet. There's
the view of nuclear stacks
from when he memorized
the alphabet front to back.
He's not doing so well.
He's doing just fine, thanks.
He's stuck between U
and double U
and the cheerleaders refuse
to spell out his name.
The lake sun sets like a
victory parade float,
he's always thought so.
Not everything will change
tomorrow. Cheerleaders
practise inverted vees
on the painted grass –
so he imagines, on hands
and knees, combing his fingers
through cerulean shag.
Hear that? That's a fleet
of beetles on bottlecaps
striking out for Kincardine.
The current does its thing,
and when he leaves
he'll leave to a hero's welcome.

From the Outside In

Underdone funeral parlour, floral
papered walls in colours clinically proven
to soothe, I'm moved to watch my second hand
sack-hop ahead. Galileo lit on the pendulum clock
in an oak-backed pew, a blessed Renaissance breeze
swung the cathedral's chandelier in periods
counted out with his pulse: *one* censer, *two* censer ...
Our dead friend didn't specialize, loved music:
from overhead speakers 'November Rain'
dusts eight-by-tens framed for the lobby's
Pledged surfaces. Kleenex is weapon of choice
for the meek, the earth four billion years young,
home to the deceased for forty-two of them. Questions
like Fedex packages no one's willing to sign for –
it goes without saying chronometers
have skewed our reckoning of a good life,
panels and panels of Charlie Brown
consumed by good grief. A Planck time interval
is so vapour-thin there's no before or after,
no report to follow the starter's pistol,
no revenge to bury Macbeth, no sketch artists.
The finer we measure the present, the wilder
our stab at the future; plans are thus afoot
to lower into the paunch of a desert mountain
a sixty-foot clock some optimists have designed
to last 10,000 years. You couldn't engineer
a denouement sweeter than this peach punch
or the munchkin under the table in Sunday best
munching on a gherkin. Kids are always
proud of their age, this one's about four

revolutions around a sun in a solar system
stubbornly self-centred. Galileo died under house arrest,
refusing to endorse notions that the universe
means us. Ten millennia hence, whatever creatures
scamper on prehensiles down eroded inclines
in the geopolitical state once called Nevada
will witness our final sputter like the raspberry
from a New Year's noisemaker. I overhear
a truism shared by the four-year-old's mother:
her quavering voice the hinge on the afternoon,
a jewellery box lined with black velvet.
The breadth between feeling and knowing
like chestnut and koan, or going, going
and gone. How normal he was, good heart
but bad ticker. A lesson to think on later
when resuming my daily chores, shedding Man
Ray tears, mowing tighter and tighter rectangles
towards the middle of Kentucky blue.

Re the Individual
Well-Being

for Ken Babstock

Recumbent; an IV line hitches me to vertical
        by a single vein. RNs in blue rustle up firewood,
their voices patched as if through dispatch
        where Tagalog, possibly Hindi, is the rule.

I'm calm, I'm nowhere I haven't gone before,
        and across heat-stretched rock the yellow flight
on the EKG scouts concentrations of methane
        in the slope mine of my heart. Too much? Too

much. General – no, *blanket* contrition, for a string
        of acts of omission that imagination has scared
into memory. Experience is elusive; to identify
        pain as phantom spares you none of its throb.

Dear anesthesiologist, I'm willing to forget more
        than OR lights swelling into pulsar or if you prefer
remember less. Who hasn't pretended to slump
        asleep, carried in from the car in Dad's arms

and been told later you were 'dead to the world.'
        Birdie unseen inside the computer screen though
your chirping's so caustic it ignites a plug
        of gunpowder, blunderbuss flash and I'm

the sound wave catching up, lapping propofol
          as it shorts out sodium channels. Today maybe
I awake mid-surgery, immobile, Rachmaninoff on
          the iPod dock, tincture of iodine like the mark of

plague on my ribcage. By any stretch we have it good
          and I am thankful. I say this uncertainly because
it feels like rain, time to latch windows and
          rescue laundry before the flood comes slippery

with leeches. Penny-ante reasons for unhappiness;
          shameful when my friend on the court steps sits
knees to her chest, distraught, and I crack wise,
          welcome the manhole drawing me in, wrists first,

or is it a yawning copperhead to ingest my body
          whole, lying in full sigh on the operating table
and keen for the moment's (any moment now)
          small-bore dart. One of these is a last thought.

Standard care means I undergo repairs neither
          earned nor essential, performed by trapeze artists
always gauging distance to ground. Each handclap
          flies through air. B minor. *Agnus Dei*. Bach? Bach.

The Prefab Man

Rank-and-file decisions rule the day,
my gut waves its fronds like bladderwrack
aching for rain. It's bright as a lark
outside the barbershop's wall of windowpanes,
and by any stretch I'm *here*, staring at my exact-
ness. Probable paths are both imaginary and real,
like those complex numbers whose special FX
allow functions to function, hair growth
as predictable as little league sports,
individual strands the width of oh-so-close.
Hugh Everett spent a lifetime curating paper trails
for the Weapons Systems Evaluation Group,
his one scientific contribution 8,000 words
crossing t's in the theory of many-worlds. Boot
put to bucket lists, screws to contender status –
in each parallel universe shimmers a greener
shade of green. What gene, like The Clapper
toggling open/closed circuitry in bedroom lights,
decides after so many uneventful years I need
hair in my ears? *Why me* is a branch of ontology
made cool by that guy on YouTube
who took a snapshot of every meal he ate
for eighteen months, a montage of plates and
takeout wrappers set to the chanting that fuels
your average wedding conga line.
Two kinds of people traffic the internet:
1) those who properly chew their food, 2) those
who buy sandwiches from vending machines
and dream of Ray Bradbury. Soviets in the seventies
landed the first unmanned lunar rover;

engineers bunkered inside a Ukranian mine
sweated the three-second delay from joystick
to action response. I'd started for my front door
before I thought *haircut*, long before my gaze
came to accept this mirror's frame,
subroutines in the brain Xing out
an ad hoc gameplan, a final oral flourish:
'The no-fuss bedhead, please.'
Everett was a three-pack-a-day man, he quit
more than once – the Hugh who succumbed each time
just happened to be our-universe Hugh.
Doesn't matter what style I choose,
some double has dogged me to a shadow bar,
bought me a tequila sunrise, made peace
over minor differences in perspective
and shared a polite groan about the tourists.
The barber folds down the collar of
my plastic cape. *Electric razor* becomes
the simplest explanation for that smooth sensation
on a neck now charged with propping a top
lousy with come-hither, like the Cold War moon.

Flight of the
Mild-Mannered

Suds froth on the wipers
as two rag-clothed arms whump the car door.
Smash cut to: chassis under a February false spring
spanked with hot wax from a non-contiguous
quicksilver past. Cut back to:
water blast *gah*ing the driver-side window.
My limbic system's convinced of a happy ending
ever since it made a unilateral decision
to pay an extra $3.99 for a finish
too good for a clunker like mine.
Futureward travel is a makeable putt.
To arrive younger than I'd otherwise be,
like outweighing gravity, or peeling shine off a trophy.
Tires nudge into stage two, spittle hits the windshield,
tentacles lower onto the hood –
an old man-o'-war gumming down soup.
I raise the traveller to my lips, sound out a sip.
My pathways log double-double good,
flood with dopamine and hope
that there's enough thrust in the blow and glow
to warp my world line, bend me and my Hyundai
out of time. It's only human to see
the universe as adversary.
Three minutes in this tunnel lost
before rinsewater drops manage to reverse
their usual course, scurry northward over glass.
A marvel. That counts as a thought
worth halving, cracking rock against rock
within earshot of grown-up voices

and the *sfft* of stubbies into Styrofoam cozies.
Inside each rock a fortress of solitude.
That's me under the deck: smooth arms, baby teeth.
What can I say? Knowing
where it ends, up ahead, a square of sun
in a mineral city that'll disappoint him.
The banner hung above the exit
begins with a cursive *Please*,
gavel-raps into all-caps, DO NOT BRAKE!
Asks me to wait until after release, gate lift.
No mention of acceleration, speed limit,
foley artist hunched over a singing saw
behind the cinder-block wall, awaiting his cue: *flying car*.
You and I, kid, we'll come together anew
into the brave. My laugh lines in the rear-view
mimic Minkowski diagrams
from orbital socket to cheekbone.
My vehicle's grille breaks the invisible plane.

Double Windsor

Flip the tips of your collar,
                     lean into the throttle.

Draw the wide end longer,
                     ring the cathedral bell.

Pull up through the loop,
                     stuff the suggestion box.

Swing round to the stoop,
                     pick up fair Goldilocks.

Overshoot the guardrail,
                     wriggle out of the noose.

Slip away from the funeral,
                     wear your double loose.

Paleosubwoofer

A pounding synth in my brain stem.
Last night's Merlot? Or some amphibian vestige?
That I feel anything approaching four-four time
is a triumph of psyche over busyness
that sees me shower, tousle, shave,
decide on khaki and a V-neck, push LIQUEFY
on the blender and click through
the closing Nikkei, Shanghai and Hang Seng,
my button-fly pressing against countertop granite
a billion years old – all before
oh-eight-hundred. So says the thirty-two kilohertz
remarkably conserved beneath my watch's face.
Semisoft, lukewarm tumescence heralds
an auspicious market opening, not much else:
a day of fill or kill, low-maintenance interface
with baristas, adrenaline rabbit run.
That ache between the shoulder blades
as though my Barbie box were yanked:
'Math is hard.' Easy enough to say.
Red and green US$ rounded to the hundredth place
butterfly and back-crawl across my screen,
homunculus in my laptop
hauling number cards as big as brontosaurus paws
the length of the scoreboard.
Readily distracted, I hop wireless zones
across the downtown core, jockey for chitchat.
Lunch at noon sharp: bean salad, for the antioxidants.
Forty's the standard candle of physicals,
of earning power and sexual regret.
Forty puts the lie to club soda with gentle dabs, tropical fish

as pets, high-interest savings accounts.
Hume starts making sense: no one
can guarantee the sun's rise, not even orphans
with hole-punched eyes. Should I
sell short or buy long? Natural markers dissemble
like AM radio under the overpass,
yesterday as material as my first recollection,
age two and a half, index finger tracing
the faux chinoiserie on Mum's vanity.
Memory's laminar flow,
parting waves of loss and gain. Like the tug
as steel runners groove into friction, then release.
Or a signature move in super slo-mo,
passage so tactile it's Braille. Day traders,
close your eyes to it.
Brief nostril flex as lungs fill,
the espresso machine's *tsk, tsk*
then glottal stop. Fillips within the darkness.
A MIDI chord vibrates on down the axon line.

En Passant

The post-coital cigarette has made a comeback
with the younger set, trimming your pubes
de rigueur for either sex, my doing so
renders me that much older for the attempt,
smoke hanging like tinsel in the indoor
winter gloom. Those Russians. Nabokov,
a master in literary circles, was a club player
in the chess world; his quirks, their spin and charge,
rendered meaningless by the board. Adulterers
sweat the ordinary, duck down hallways while
mores like capuchin monkeys chatter coyly and eye
their wallets. Once you've done the unexpected,
she becomes again a twentysomething with punk ethic
and pink streak, fetching if unconvincing. Critical scenes
from Lang's *Metropolis* have since gone missing,
they've tidied up the plot with intertitles
in a smooth typeface. Cerebellum, a babel
of turbines spitting out mouthfuls of steam and steel
hairballs. Her cat that drops from the mantle
ain't the same cat that lands, its molecular makeup
a quantum frappé, you can't draw an equal sign
between any particle-then and particle-now.
I've tried to hide my bald spot with ballcap,
paunch with high-waisted jeans, 'Be all you can be'
a tautology as tireless as the special-needs teacher
I hastily married. In 2005 some grad student
at MIT flicked on fluorescent lights
in a gymnasium festooned for the first-ever
Time Traveller Symposium, figuring a firm date
plus psychedelic poster would lure them out.

His two roommates showed up drunk, and late.
Define *clock* and I'll let you have my cake,
a tradition on birthdays, the number of candles
over the years tactfully dwindling like ticks on
a lemming. Consciousness, that 'ominous, ludicrous
luxury' says the man who gave us Lolita
and wilful perversion made art; do I
break it off for good or go for one more romp?
Grot, foreman of the Heart Machine,
hauled on his beard as the caterwauling mob
pressed up the steps to jam its hydraulics, Fritz's future
a deco glory in dayshift black and white.
I once towered over common sense
but no longer possess the brainpower
to link my younger protagonist with the one here
on the editing room floor. Too-human eyes
sacrifice truth for sequence, advance me a single
square at a time, beside her, ball joint to hip
in a room veered dystopian with morning.

Two

That Stratospheric Streak
My Green Filament

A.M.

Leafless season, the tallest cedars
like stags knocking antlers.
The initial ordered state creates history:
pell-mell drifts down, vibrations in air become sound.
Just left of the sternum I find my echo.
Short ride out to the fence,
long walk back, flickering like a nickelodeon.
Milkweed pods have given their lives for my childhood good.
Childhood god? TV Tarzan.

Sprayed intermittently on trunks, hunter-orange I's
like radioactive keyholes.
Some would choose great strength for their special power,
others incredible speed or x-ray vision.
I halt and take in how loud, clumsy, unmistakable I've been.
Wherever I am now
becomes in retrospect my yellow sun.
Clear-cut the colour of darkroom fixer,
I never spot the deer, only the deer's afterimage.

A.M.

These days without sequence.
Static from the drag of Nikes through yellow maple leaves.
I've no place to be
and make out clearly the space-time grid
around the child in the playground.
All light's invisible, otherwise we couldn't see,
the next wave in the series already en route.
That man with galoshes slouches like my father.
Boy on a see-saw like a bubble in a flute.

Near the park an electrified squirrel, pole high,
spread-eagle in the breeze.
Look down: on the sidewalk, flattened gum, a scratched-out smiley face.
Irony in antiphony.
Remove the abstract
and all sympathy is self-evident.
Skirmishes continue across the blood-brain barrier.
Other squirrels, lockstep with the cold, skittish as errand itself:
        insistent, incomplete.
Me, itching for the live wire.

P.M.

Proprioceptors ravelled into a Gordian knot –
the decisive clue that you may've woken from a long nap
like a finch flying through dry ice.
Every direct ancestor, for me to be alive,
found a way to procreate.
I've no workable umbrella,
take my first-ever date to the laser show.
Fixtureless horizon and Darwin seasick for months below deck,
pining for the gentle roll of his daily walk.

My psychopomp a hare set on its ear.
That's my hand, my finger next to hers
tracing circles on the armrest's soft pile.
Where is she now?
We touch, we touched, like loops of a lemniscate.
No love left,
but time spent together is imprinted,
a fossil with clear antecedents.
In the sketchbook a Galapagos tortoise stares out from behind
its likeness.

P.M.

I've no gold wings
but I have a goose egg
from *the landing, thank god* or that's a long flight to the bottom
stair.
Headlong into accidentally on purpose.
Indoor sledding's a game for Romanovs and show-offs.
Whether it just looks like me, my double maybe,
where I sprawl now.
Brown vinyl runner nailed to the staircase
like the mud trail of some animal dragged to the bush.

From side door to backyard pool like the Flash his legs over the
        weed-rippled flagstone.
Mortar in ever-present crumble,
but why would he notice it?
My eyes, his legs,
the track becomes a record of history.
Cannonball or jackknife – he does both and splits worlds.
Splash hovers, a glass crown
whose light goes out
as it crashes over the concrete deck.

A.M.

Authorized Personnel Only, the sign says.
Across alkali flats through saltbush the wind throws voices.
Oppenheimer stretches to full height, alone,
walks as I walk
into the unrepentant heat.
I record data for playback, including desert crust
displaced by the toe of my boot.
We've no centre,
only sides to consider, moving towards or away from either.

Mantis-eyed aliens these days with their expectant looks.
The auburn outline of my hand
tells me where I am
when I hold that hand to the zenith.
Sand shot up, trinitite funnelled down while the barracks expand
    with that big band sound.
The flash reaches everyone everywhere
at the same time.
A choir of green balloons
over the last fill-up for miles, nodding in the fumes.

P.M.

Goes the gate, *knock knock.*
Goes the gate in the rainstorm,
boy asleep behind a night-lit window.
Where am I now, old lady?
Yodel lay he who.
The mattress kicks back, he wakes from a lucid fall
with a bellyful of fear.
We might claim history had unfolded.
Thick with dog-ears, *More Adventures of the Great Brain* slides from
    pillow to parquet.

Describe the room,
an amalgam of bedrooms for the ideal child:
a double-page spread from a Sears catalogue.
White walls resolve into perfect-bound corners.
Discrete breaths under the Spider-Man bedsheet,
a cobweb in the breeze.
Entirely shadow, I stand tall
behind the closet door left ajar.
The subject proves computationally intractable.

P.M.

Like a winched submersible
passing depth levels purple to yellow.
I sleeve off window fog into a streaky ampersand –
where are we now?
As likely Hokkaido as Helsinki, Oslo as Irkutsk.
Behind the taps, silverware clanks glass, sword on shield.
Perpetually between, the ferry lowers its gangplank
with a tiny boom.
Sea spray rises a half step, sharp.

On the return I treat myself to a pint of plain.
Stare at the long eye in the spinning bucket of water,
tip myself in.
I've no more kronor.
In timber churches Greenland Norse refuse to fish
while their herd dwindles hillside.
Threadbare, they sing.
Among the favoured I'm indistinguishable.
Mainland recedes and the old-growth forests that we have are all
    we have.

P.M.

Along the wall of guitars sunlight plays straw-coloured strings.
The bodies gleam, *don't touch me*:
a Visigoth strung up by his neck.
Delight worms from dread,
my alter ego insists we've seen one before.
The girl in my peripheral, she's beautiful.
A garland tattoo curls over her collarbone.
Our eyes widen as the horde rushes towards
where we stand now.

I've no defences
against the pinwheel spin.
Julius Caesar pads 46 BC with two extra months, *carpe diem* by decree.
The cupbearer boy brandishes a stalk, asks: 'Bush or tree?'
It does not seem outlandish.
The only hope for control is to plot
a triumphant return.
On the walk home I become a figment in shop windows,
coat pocket jangling, keys and change.

A.M.

Hour of the MuchMusic logo,
my black Chucks straddle the bagged *Star* glittery with dew.
Shallow breaths before
imminent click of the rusty screen door.
Undetected so far from rec room to front steps,
underneath her parents' second-floor window.
Insert girlfriend's name here.
I've come through the night ridden into intact.
Dashing home polysyllabic like relief through a front-tooth gap.

My shoestring ends fray at an imperceptible rate.
Overgrown fields sprout new residential blocks,
sun lollygagging over the same rise
where I pause now.
A river of attention laid down over a river.
Top-heavy with exhaustion, briefly I'm aware
I've no centre.
Greying and slippered, I descend cream-carpeted stairs,
happy but no wiser.

P.M.

Down by the way, where the watermelon sings,
where I do not know.
Do I remember the words,
do the words remember me?
Pages turn themselves in the librarian's lap, or
a butterfly on a twig suns its wings.
My son in the rear-view buckled up for our detour.
Speeding past the old street: gone the creek,
gone the creek's frogs after school.

Dashboard gauges twitch as pressure climbs.
Like dye in the brain, the vapours of the downtown core.
Descent into the Bay Area, that's me,
a cameo
by aircraft porthole.
Overhead light on and on, still on.
He can't see himself but I can.
He focuses on the wing's bank into the cloud chamber.
He has no son.

A.M.

Heavy-duty staples split the grain of utility poles.
Staples rusted to a stampede of buffalos.
Every thing is meticulously present.
This story of history has no outcome
because it has no motion.
If t is represented by the horizontal axis: staples like pairs of alleles.
Concrete poured into the shape of curbs.
Electromagnetic signals
spider across northern skylines.

Mist in suspension over the sewer grate,
the winter queen of subterranean 3-space.
Green traffic light is a multifaceted green.
'Are you the postulate?' the city asks.
Matter is merely borrowed and with visible breath I reply,
'I've no centre.'
If it were necessary to tell someone where I am,
I'd say the spheres of Kepler resonate like icicles.
I'd say I have loved.

Three

Suede Spats

Your strawberry banana shake.
My root beer float, the cross-section
where sassafras and vanilla equilibrate.
Our booth's mini jukebox hoards static
while Marilyn peddles pouts above Arborite –
flecks of panned gold on off-white.
DuPont's Freons continue to pop O_3.
Noise radiates from the blender, on/off
behind the counter, a metronome
pacing our latest squabble. You ask how it all started
and I belt out 'Dunno' with the certainty of a bass
doo-wopping the close.
You insist, so okay, here goes:
13.7 billion years ago, before she blows,
the universe is a restive place.
A witness stand, Trojan horse, comma splice.
Come, let's watch the kettle drum,
forces run-tap-tapping the periodic table
to fire up the nuclear furnace.
Leave off worries of harness and hubris
on Bathtub Row, crude oil, tectonic plates,
supernovas unspooling their life-giving goo.
Just take in the minimalism: one stock forty-watt
and a Brechtian broom.
Sorry, there's no time to apologize.
That's matter in the wings, scaling
an oscillogram, stretching a hamstring,
ready to hammer-throw spirals, ellipses, peculiars:
galaxies fanning out like patches on denim.
Now knock together a spindle cell or three

and crystal-ball your porous, mostly electrolyte claim
on three dimensions. I'll do the same.
Imagine them entwined, leg over leg
in morning sun. What a moron the heart is.
I stage-whisper 'smithereens,' reach for your hand,
a comfort when confronting the curtain rise
on megacosm. Moonshine whistle triggers
salivary glands and what's that taste?
Black licorice?
Begin-time blasts us apart.
Whoosh go my drip-bag isms,
litotes, wisecracks, the godfather of particle colliders
depositing me this far, no farther,
to high-step in front of my parade. You,
swiftly from Hox genes to daytripper,
trail heat across the snow globe
and rack up minor victories
given the statistically significant chance
we meet, double-spoon a sundae, clock
our amazement at the non-repeat sequence
of monthly flavours. A joy not possible
before the big bang made creation some sweet place.

Inflatable Moat

Picture a Bundt cake with centre hole
shiny enough to suggest *crown*. I won't
be tempted. I'm an honest dissembler
with responsibilities, of good standing
in my demesne. Just last month I foiled

another attempt on the sovereign's life
with a turkey baster and some Muenster.
Details are classified but keep in mind
I'm handy in the scullery. Food-taster's
stressful work, I had early in my career

a public falling out with the court jester:
stabbed him with a meat thermometer.
That was my first promotion. Sous-chef.
An onion peeled for every thumped rat,
their eyes dim with the future to be had –

is that me, swaddled in a grand carriage
between county estates, king of my own
catering company? Indeed, the envoy
gallops over the rise, table's set, and I've
a fancy new hat. Ready the drawbridge!

Heads We Win,
Tails You Lose

My butt all bone against curb, I'm anxious for
the golf cart's cushion, clubs tipped over on the lawn
like a giant squid autopsy in progress. By and large,
cephalopods are smart enough to stay wet.
First rule of survival: pick your battleground.
Most protomammals went inland, others
did a one-eighty, dunked back under, lost their hard-
won legs jogging by in lavender hot pants ...
She's immaterial to the issue at hand:
whales, only hours to save them, harpooning
banned in 1986, superseded on the sly. Surprise
surprise, Japan and Norway, two countries
I've either visited or would like to again.
Terra firma has its pluses. Minuses include
the petrified huddle in wine cellars at Pompeii
that Picasso took a pass on as tableau; the thought
of the skeleton cupping her toddler's skull
could scoop out your heart if you let it.
Bunkers a.k.a. sandtraps are a cinch
to hit, they crackle in midday like tinfoil.
Iceland's overrun with health nuts despite
the literacy rate, my twosome buddy swears
that on islands the rehydrating's faddish.
A Jeremiah with his irons, more obtuse than acute,
he mans a vehicle with a sizable trunk.
Water can be a hazard too, as when Vesuvius lit up
like a question mark and the pyroclastic wave
vaporized H_2O molecules in every body
turned glyph. Lilac for the girl's pants, I amend

my original assessment. So many things can go wrong
when you swim recreationally in the ocean,
that's why I haven't. Take the USS *Indianapolis*,
Robert Shaw by all accounts ad libbing
'Farewell and adieu to you, ladies of Spain' –
that was sharks but medium's the same, amplifying
military sonar, forcing our cetacean cousins
to choose sides, some ramming astray
onto shores of particulate glass. Obsidian's black
obscures the violets crucial for its form
in temperatures of hundreds of degrees.
Always late for tee-off, doofus cradles dirty looks
when denied the right to play through,
my fingers crossed for a cooler, uneventful round.
Stencilled on a dinghy, *Greenpeace* shatters spray,
beads the lens, handicam with jerky frame
separating whaler from prize. I mean *violence*,
the roar loosened when we score a hole in one.

Regular Folks
Going Bananas

What's it been? Four days,
four solid-colour ties in shades of grey,
your expression coached to an innocence
consistent with your attorney's
alternate theory of the crime. Now and then
I notice you flag under the strain of such phlegm –
you know me as juror number nine.
Number ten's nodding off again, eyeframes
on a saliva-white string looped nape to bosom.
My leg's racketing a heel in rhythm
to second-per-second flow of the dreamable;
on my pad I doodle a time machine:
knob and tube, dual exhaust, Barcalounger.
Walkie-talkie com system,
weigh-scale antipendulum drive.
Counsel and the aggrieved continue to
agreeably disagree, every other statement held up
like stained glass to the actionable past
in a rundown of testimony from MM/DD/YY.
Court reporter, jam-eyed,
setting upon the stenotype as though rappelling a cliff,
judge humped with news of a month to live
while tumbleweeds of O_2
trip a saturation level near minimum
for us civil twelve to reckon reasonable doubt.
Counterfactuals pile up like cornflakes pile up
like models of megamolecules, a witness pointing out
you wouldn't've candlesticked anyone
in kitchen, study or Kensington co-op

if the rage never 'occurred.'
Number six, our foreperson (self-appointed),
a grade-school teacher punchy with the week's pass,
records it all with bubblewrap script
on double-lined notepaper, your certain guilt
the keel that keeps her lungs afloat.
Sorry for that.
Sorry to get hopped up on danish and OJ in breakroom
and whang stereotypes around.
You'd twirl your pencil stash to hear how fast
we brachiate from *if* to *hell yeah*.
Bemoaning the long hours, we'll punish you
for what we've more or less lost.
So trust me, I'm onside when your attorney,
an afternoon into appealing for discovery
of new facts, stumbles on the grandfather paradox
as an airtight defence. If you did arc the hammer
into your good neighbour's jaw
and subsequently robbed Peter to pay Paul,
how could Spock ever have been born
to cover that tune? Humming *all over this la-a-and*,
I return to the present, mildly hypoxic,
staggered with mistrials.

Baffle Gate

Pay no mind to the postdoc salting celery
or that row of Bunsen burners, beakers
      flanking the karaoke bar.

Looks like your basic turnstile, up on blocks.
It's not, in the way a contour line is not
      Napoleon on the march.

At six o'clock: chevrons in reflective tape.
The ramp for our subject's giddy-up
      into bird's nest soup.

I said flywheel. You vector from trouble here,
exit through inclement weather. Set theory
      codifies free will.

We've placed betas in metros, in libraries,
in wonderlands and misty monasteries
      purpled under guy wires.

You have choices to make. So make them.
After each one, the thunk of a dynamo
      with arms of chrome.

Size Extra Medium

My favourite T-shirt reads *Same Shit,*
Different Pile; it says I'm a fun guy
but only reflects the inner me the moment
I start wearing it to bed. Third visit to
the sleep clinic plays out as punchline ... I see
there's a polygraph lying on the floor. *Ba dum chhh.*
Someone in the next room's peeing again,
that porcelain bowl huzzah. The perimeter to the diameter
became 'pi' just before the Industrial Revolution
introduced canaries to coal mines;
no one got much shut-eye then, especially the
nimbler children. Your Own Personal O_2 Bar
would've been worth its weight while leading
a purblind pony into a seam – some shiny thing
to rejuvenate you on a cellular level,
its silent compressor with baffler a new world
novelty. I've memorized to a hundred digits
the non-repeating random walk of π
in hopes that the heat off my CPU
melts the melatonin in my pineal gland. Waffles
with butter are better than waffles without,
breakfast for insomniacs a mélange of dread
and relief. The Brain Wave, as seen on TV,
is a device that massages your scalp
with oscillating finger wires and 'must be felt
to be believed.' To have dreamwork etched
by polysomnogram requires some electrodes glued
to your temple, behind your ears, and tubes
up your nose. EKG leads on my chest dive into
a flight recorder on the night table, in case

I arrive morningside with my charred body
several cornfields away from my wings.
Most numbers are angels, inexpressible
as fraction. Rational approximation
is both how we make major decisions and why
they're so often wrong, longing for patterns
because we've lost the means to live restfully
without code. It's somewhere around
pi's billionth placeholder that you find
eight eights in a row, like pellets of a mole rat.
Cryptographers toss and turn over advances
in quantum computers that'll harness like a rodeo clown
laughter and its otherworld interference –
the gibbous moon beyond the roped-off curtain
an open-mouthed grin. In addition to
power on/off, volume up, volume down,
channel up and down, it's a solace to know
the World's Simplest Remote includes mute.

Carbon Monoxide,
Alka Seltzer and the
Slow Pitch of Acceptance

I know your now-husband
like I know Altoids' unholy smoulder
on my tongue. In black tails, he turns out tall,
a square shooter, gut proud, premature baldness
compensated for by guffaws
plus goatee. His one-two punch of girth and mirth
makes him a prize specimen of sexual dimorphism,
a fearsome receiving-line end.
Your suffix for Saturdays to come: able.
As in hug and amen, ply and stuff.
'Marriage-worthy,' my wife whispered
to hush me mid-ceremony.
I hadn't spoken: under canopy fringe and ion charge
down cumulus hills, roughened by gusts off
the eighteenth green, a thought bubble
soft-boiled the words *fair* and *way*, is all.
How germane to the exchange of vows
cueing your Act II; the unheralded high-voltage zig
in upper spheres; the mean free path
of the career-wise thirtysomething.
Inside the hall, your whitened smile
is eclipsed by the tapered occiput of the guy
weight-shifting in front of me,
a rawboned stiff out of keeping with the revelry,
esp. with buffet lids tilted on the side wall
like hubcaps on display.
The man's dark grey, Tip Top fabric. Dandruff

erecting a megalith along his collarbone
as air kiss after kiss
soar like helicopters over your cheeks.
Welcomes, congrats, O happy days.
We come to worship a fixed earth
in league with sailors at sea, Spanish caravels
billowing towards a horizon of finite regress –
which at least licences the belief
we're making progress
towards that first twist-off at the open bar.
Without time's invisible framework
I'd never pool tomorrow in my hotel bed
like heavy water, fazed by another night squandered
after a charming number of imports, domestic premiums,
then sad Coors Lights. And you'd never
fork a hubby more deli-style dill than bread-and-butter
if you didn't believe you could change him.
If you didn't feel change in yourself.
Unchecked mitosis can't be your only excuse
for a move like this, a lonely testament
to so much pressed linen.
Don't get me wrong, cuz, when you unwrap
the CO detector, I wish you nothing
but good news, monthly readouts in parts per million
well within acceptable range.
My gift detects cause for regret.
It's not the ceiling that spins; it's your head.

Nine Exes in a Silo, Pt. 1

Does anybody love anybody anyway?
— Howard Jones

She reclines
in a high-backed seat
bunkered deep on the Pilates Coast,
launch button a clown nose on the pope.

From your porch swing you watch a frog
leap towards a mosquito. It winks …
the *mosquito* winks.
Frog's tongue
a jet of ink tagging its rear end.

Remember the tailor
who took in her slacks?
The neighbour's Corgi rolling in the grass.
It was just you and her, in underthings, feeling for
silver cuff links in the dark.
After the punch bowl knuckled into the dirt.
After she swore, you swooned.

Whose limo driver with the crystal ear?
Whose rhumb line ends in a shopping cart?
Her polarizing effect on city lights
left you a hillbilly tossing pearl onions
like shurikens.
The *hillbilly* was, understand.

She passed on the franks 'n' beans,
printed her own currency.
Had a fortress built on Skype Island

and lived with a cherry orchard
growing in one hemisphere or the other –

Because it's never anybody's fault.
The smoothest stones for skipping still sink.
Because every episode ends with burnt toast.

Anyway, now she wants you to see her
in her daughter.
You've never really learned
how to properly pack a parachute.
Just who does she think she is, the daughter?
Smiling into the surveillance camera,
rainbow-coloured braces the final word on
badminton in the Olympics.

Absence redresses the excluded middle.
After every birth, *somebody* pauses,
wrists deep in suds.
Field after field of hoofbeats.
Phosphorescent mobile over the drumlin,
horns in the offing.

Anybody rates scattered applause.

You go about the day, you must,
adjusting your bearing as necessary
whenever you hear an errant shuttlecock
hiss into Mandolin Lake.

In Thunderation

Sandwiched between trailer and feature, a comet
heads for earth while field phones in the front lines
muddy meadow grasses. How about some tongue
before magma reaches the beaches of Normandy

and I'll score you popcorn with extra butter oil,
maybe a bottomless soda. Thursday's flying now.
The photogenic couple behind us bought their tix
online, they've a two-year-old with cystic fibrosis

in a house made of gold tinfoil. Backstory porn –
hell, *nobody* makes out in theatres anymore. U-boat
in scale with a child's monster hand, the shutter
bags the money shot, bubbles fly past portholes

like blond locks in Ken's convertible. Quite a pair
on our hometown sheriff! Or subaltern, whatever
Hanoi Jane stitched atop a gun turret signifies.
Buddy from Arkansas under full moon, dog tag as

crucifix, billet-doux in bloody paws. Soldiers glide
through winter wheat. Rows back they're going at it
like D-listers making for shore. We munch in unison,
invested in her muffled cries. As she crests, he dies.

Adventure
Chemistry Set

If motion is an illusion stitched together
by brains too rushed for a proper breakfast,
the home-security racket has recently duped
our PTA. Photocells like W. C. Fields
squint from detector mounts; fence to fence
I'm the adult supervision stamping out lengths
in perpetuity on lunch-hour duty.
Sixth grade I was a Jedi master with a
pronounced overbite, Jerry Lewis and his kids
were collecting dimes on TV – there's nothing wrong
with growing up that a cool nickname
can't fix. Now like then, violence solves for x
in the schoolyard, faces look up at my approach,
show their work feigning innocence:
'Aw, wasn't doing anything, Mr. T!'
Paul Ekman spent years in Papua New Guinea
as the white man with gadgets; surprise, he says,
is impossible to fake, even for a bully
not yet zit-flecked. As designated grown-ups,
teachers accrue a royal retinue, keeners mostly,
until the chimes of the autobell. When out of order
we dust off those bronze hand-held clappers
and let fly. Happiness has a distinct musculature,
I imagine my mug from that other time
shown to a tribesman leaning on his staff.
He's content with what the world shows him,
his rods and cones like loose change
thrown on the communal bill. Effectively blind

forty minutes each day, the human eye
acts to minimize blur, not lying to us per se
but operating on your basic 'need to know.'
The way one deflects questions in the staff room
mornings after another eHarmony disaster show
at Jack Astor's. The in-crowd's at it again,
playing keep-away with Hamlet's sock toque,
that treble cry ringing out across decades:
'Uncle!' I am your Horatio, Luke,
wearing out battlements, the ghost of lessons past
on rotary – the way magnesium combusts
makes for a most impressive science class.
Though prescreened for ownership of more than
two cats, for walks in the fucking *rain*,
by dinner's end my date had gunned through
all six of Ekman's so-called primary emotions
like a dirt bike in a motordrome. Sadness
twice. Dreams, I tell my kids, are the universal acid
nothing can contain. Ages four through thirteen,
they honk like geese under a birdless sky
while cloud-roll folds their recess into mine.

International
Date Line

'Flyboy, toss over that ratchet wrench,'
said the chronobiologist to the relief pilot
who'd spend all day tomorrow on the couch
after a second hissy fit threw his back out.

Lubricant pooled sheen on the concrete.
Happy couples flocked to its coastline,
set up umbrellas, fed each other crudités
and wantonly flouted the seatbelt sign.

'Honest, yesterday it worked just perfect,'
the pilot moaned to the gals, straps undone,
backsides up following a frolic in the surf.
He'd forgotten to turn on the intercom.

The chronobiologist tapped the armature
with a hammer the pilot had handed him:
'This here's your problem. It's crepuscular,
naturally the gloomiest light for a solo man.'

Lurching upright, the pilot rocked the cockpit:
'I won't land her till I catch the setting sun!'
It sounded petulant, like a statement of fact.
He tried once again and slipped on the ocean.

Four

Trust Fund

Brother and sister watch the estate lawyer
take a cork-backed ruler to the ground plan –

two wings behind a cast iron gate, a barn
raised for the Shetlands. Into the picture

flock grouse, the furious Vs breed Ws,

while on the French-curved cobbled path
a litter of kittens cascades in a burlap sack.

Brother and sister like stowaways clasp hands
as the horizon lifts and blackens the moor.

Mother in whalebone from her boudoir

warned she'd return every seventeen years
with the locusts. Since they first sat down,

the antique globe on the lawyer's desk
has not stopped spinning Pacific, Pacific.

Testosterone
Anonymous

Our duck caller over open water trumpets
a world that ends not in fire but rubber.
Sighting along the barrel, I estimate
thirty yards to the decoy spread, suitably weighted
for a morning layered to the stratosphere
with foreboding. What we measure twice is absolute;
what we free pour is Absolut. We're LLBS
of Queen's on a biennial retreat, our nostalgia
like the white paste on a geisha. Doubling
every known thing in the universe means doubling
the ruler too: nebulas, monster home runs,
your prick whether flaccid or erect –
thus no boon to the teenager you were
Saturday nights with the girlfriend, back seat
in the family Caravan, mapping its vinyl faults
while power ballad spun into new wave.
Our parietal lobe plays director, framing shots
in out-of-body experiences, so who's to say
what commands my visuospatial sense
when I shoot and miss the pillowy hen breast
in its wheel over the Catherine moor.
Those spells spent behind the locked
bathroom door, I just don't have plan or prayer
in me anymore, the weft of migratory flock
a banshee grooving to those dark
dancehall days. Kant's 'island universes'
are in fact outracing their trails of light;
future astronomers will see jack in the night sky

and conclude, based on best available data,
we are the centre. It's not that I give a fuck
about the fowl – just sunk by the here-to-thereness,
400 billion Andromedas gone like
400 billion Jimmy Hoffas in a trunk.
Some miscalculations loom larger than others,
some verdicts quick as whistle-stop puffs:
crossing the gymnasium under 'Lovesong' gusts
to talk to that button-slick girl, catching halfway there
the alarm in her eye. When a mallard's hit
it becomes projectile, a crackpot jumping off a cliff
strapped to a winged contraption. Distance
doesn't wince, the horizon's G for ground floor,
which makes my camouflaged blind an elevator.
Unseen hands pull stars from kitchen blue
like sport socks off a clothesline –
you might not believe I've a loving wife at home
but I do, I do. Slippers on, groggy with dawn,
she's an early experiment in human flight.

Growth Food

Meanwhile seems infinite,
though downtime in Terminal 1 causes *seems*
to lose its amateur status, shuck its padded helmet
and tap gloves with *is*
for fifteen rounds. Anthropologists estimate
three major life events (or equivalents)
are lost in airports, esp. for the adaptive traveller
numb to burps of fatigued steel,
epidermal cells flaking in aerosol hisses,
movator creep, strangers' sock feet.
Some prefer their symbols jumbo-sized, oversold,
Caesarean-born. Yes,
unchecked tech's *sui generis*, evident
as our numbers near … what? Seven billion?
Me, I'm cocooned in my sample size of one
by noise-cancelling headphones,
generating antigens like a coal-firing plant
while the departure lounge speeds faster than *c*
on the crest of space-time. Impossible
makes me queasy, cream-based sauces too;
both are responsible for this motion sickness,
a poorly lit video loop on a website
somewhere in my neural net.
Mind taps the aquarium glass: *don't don't don't*
and sound waves melodeon, 120 dBs or more –
a behemoth from Emirates turns heads.
Coming or going? An instant's neither.
Hung there in cruciform on unknown vector,
a giant white knuckle. Are you visualizing
deck chairs on the *Titanic*? I am

vexed by one step for a [*sic*] man
among routine leaps for species-kind.
No mistake, mobility has dubious side effects:
dodgeball, the Charleston, middle-manager career arc.
East-west goes the sun like a comb-over
fooling no one, our faces exposed
in revolving doors and dusk-darkened windows
as elevators settle floor to floor
in every city flown to or conceivable.
We live to forget. Most we can hope for is
an upgrade to executive before the very end:
interstellar sheen, virtual particles popping in, out.
Nanofluff. Deleted expletives. Sure,
let's talk late-blooming rhododendrons, queues for this
and that, climate versus weather, 'Do cats emote?'
Go ahead, luv, unload your joke
about hanky-panky when you're old.
I've got another layover in LAX.

Rolling Lock

The conference room
        on the fifty-fifth floor
with a drop-dead view.

        Briefcase hinges loose
but grimly holding out
        for fat Hansel's doom.

Nippled mannequins
        posed as accountants
and in-house counsel.

        Headless on a scaffold
two window-washers
        stand blood-stricken.

Now ten fewer seconds
        since bullet train Doppler
made the silence worse.

        Your sweatdrops course
like piranha streaming
        towards a baby heron.

The safest combination
        the one you've forgotten.

Addressing
Human Resources

I don't believe in luck, and still mine's dumb.
Ace Billy Bishop twice phoned in sick and missed
ambush by howitzer and bloodbath at the Somme.
Took out seventy-two enemy planes in the Great War
before 'skill set' became a common term;
they ask what mine is, eye my lemon suit.
Easy to overdress in the workplace during
boom times, women are allowed open-toed footwear
after May Two-Four, some don Crocs or flip-flops.
'I'm a good team player,' I repeat, flick
my Five Alive tab, wait on the next question.
Imagine: shot down by a Canadian.
Cloud cover a trap door, you clutch your number
like a chit from the bakery, instruments awhirl,
wind tuned to a concert pitch. The death spiral.
Any well-designed system is parsimonious
with expended energy, all parts give out at once
on the bottom line. My chronic body complaints
migrate shoulder to knee to lower back,
an oil glob in water, so yes, a generous
health benefits package could prove make-or-break.
Very possible my burning bush will be a stroke,
Opa almost died of one years before he died.
The wwi pilot's lifespan averaged eleven days,
spared at least the shade of cubicle grey
in my crosshairs. Billy passed away publicly blessed,
tucking into a lamb chop, patting his lips.
Genuine happiness depends on the happiness
of others; we'd gladly settle for less as long as we're

better off than our friends. Opa outlived
everyone he knew, his spine curled
to a shepherd's staff in the nursing home,
memories of his war following him in fitful
cotton bursts. Common sense puts thread count
and personal comfort in direct proportion –
I'll accept a salary commensurate with
lean-tos in Kathmandu, shantytowns in New Orleans –
there must be a thousand other things I'd rather do
with the sugar in my hourglass. Billy's MO
was to prowl the sky on rogue missions, end-run
then swoop on a dopey, green German.
Fill the theatre with bullets, sun at his back,
his victim the sole witness to the silhouette
loping like a wolf across bedsheet white
towards the call, Opa with a look in his eyes.

Fairyland

Pubescents everywhere. Down Bright Angel Trail
a field trip storms switchbacks, crowds the plateau;
parental consent slips line backpacks
like plate armour hammered to a molecular
thinness. One unlucky soul with Invisaligns
tumbles over every season, the screams unbearable
as dragons trace helical currents high above
inner spheres. Most fantasy is born of tragedy,
most death in the wild from worn-out teeth,
fossils painstakingly toothbrushed, zip-
locked into evidence. Charles Dawson,
C. D. to friends, pantsed the establishment with
an orang jaw, molars filed to mimic wear
and browned with acid: the 'missing link' assembled
(as was Adam) from a monogrammed trunk.
Grand Canyon is daunting, believe me,
the R. Colorado twinkles like faith,
the mile-deep strata an argument for floss
in variegated gummy pinks. Nana's dentures
flapped when she talked; Dad sighed and dropped
nine Gs on a new porcelain set. She, ninety-something,
greeting her chocolate Ensure each lunch
with a scabbard grin. I have to look away
when someone's daughter scampers to the edge,
dangles her legs over sandstone, conqueror at thirteen
with a recent history of three square
and promises to practice more piano.
C. D. was an amateur, swanned about afternoons
at the local, later rechristened Piltdown Man,
the workmen taking minute-hand pecks

around their ploughman's plates. Eggs, cheese, carbs,
Nana wasn't much of a cook, homemade wit
betraying her long before those dentures. Snug in
a cranny I pry off my Tupperware lid –
freshness pops out, chases a cowlick of American Spirits,
my tomato 'n' mayo sandwich says *whoa*
with Wonder Bread lips. Today's mothers
shelve recipe books on mantles alongside
Harry Potter, their kids milk-fed marvels,
ulna waved like wands over the precipice.
'Watch your footfalls near the pit, sir!'
cry the Andy-capped chaps as C. D. skulks around
to plant bones from an age before cremation.
Inheritance once meant mere continuance,
our burials modest. Dad is clean-cuffed most days,
smiles through the debt and his first
of two root canals, thankful for the anaesthesia.

Big-Game Hunters

Photons bank off the window frame, fool no one,
mere minutes on a zip line from the sun.
Slowed somewhat, it's known,
by earth's duo of nitrogen and oxygen.
Blue waves scatter – that's the answer
to your offspring's query; or the tub-thumper on pint four
fresh off a Gauloise and demanding,
'Who says my green's yours?'
Why this sky at all
is a better stab at the empirical
since we've been staring at it for an hour,
lineup accreting like an asteroid belt alongside
the shopfronts' steady-as-she-goes.
I care off and on about advancing
or staying put. Should've brought a book.
With an interlude this generous I could learn
to my capacity what there is to learn
about the 5 percent we've already worked out:
xenografts, polymers, sugar rockets.
St. John's Wort. The black arts.
Who's capable of holding but a fraction,
even less long-term? Synaptic traffic's
like having too many remotes;
why I can never remember a joke or related anecdote
to gear down on the wait, find some traction
on elbow to knuckle, rump to genital
single file. 'Excuse me,
do you have the time?' wins a look, as though I were
a giant moa, you the first Maori to climb ashore.
Everyone has a different take. Yours

off a smartphone, delivered with eyebrows raised
into single quotes. I've much more to ask. Why do we
try to contain immensities of scale
with a word like *ginormous*?
Seven million septillion stars.
A billion atoms in every sentence's full stop …
We fail together, penned on this sidewalk slab
as the noon sun Fosbury flops the daytime high.
Rising in waves off asphalt, a kelp forest.
Heat's a siren song, and my POV
wanders from mirage to memory:
church, steeple, the inside-out reveal
and wiggle of my little fingers
to represent all the people. *Look at them.*
They carousel by on bicycles, in cars, strollers, sneakers,
centring personal shells on paths sinusoidal
to avoid casual contact.
Look at us. We play our parts, manifesting
the normative attention span of a citified adult.
Neutrinos sift through our bodies to the antipodes.

Egg Timer

The girl in the booth with her back to the door
      has a boyfriend she can't forgive.
            Hollandaise sauce
            like puppy sick.
The short-order cook lives with seconds to live.

With cherry gloss in hand the girl facing out
      practises pouts into a spoon.
            Pulp freestyles
            in glassed juice.
The aging gourmand wants his eggs over soon.

From a rope off the boom mic a minature man
      drops and rolls into existence.
            Nothing new
            happens next.
A clucking hen pecks out the centre of the lens.

Primed for Contact

In our glazed bowl apples lurk as curve-
balls in pitchers' mitts, Golden Delicious
potential energy like tensed vocal cords.
Ten years of married-to, third coat of Ivory Tusk
going on kitchen walls. Pollock was much imitated
after his unqualified success, Ed Harris played him
with accordion ease in that faithful biopic;
back then modern art was projectile, plotless.
An entire Ultimate Frisbee team of hirsute,
recently matriculated engineers would hoot
at the propulsive force of a flying saucer
or any eyewitness account from a down-on-his-luck
Midwest farmer. Pocket protectors soldier on
without a peep; the Green Bank Formula
suggests inhabitable planets in numbers
that make one wonder why the night sky creaks
with satellite junk. Life forms with any autonomy
likely look familiar, say exobiologists:
open systems that fence cellular decay
with rusting rapiers. Anyone can paint, the way
anyone can swing a stick and play the xylophone.
To do it tolerably takes calluses, alone time,
comfortable shoes. I lead the roller
into the unmapped areas while radio towers
broadcast earth's position and population like a drunk
trying to corral the quietest key. What excites
the hardcore base is hope of sentient beings
fluent in abstract expressions: 'Love is
watching you peel a hard-boiled egg,' she said,

standing between me and the calendar Xs.
Jackson was an alcoholic and obscurantist,
and despite his genius couldn't hide this
from the sock-hop America he died in, age forty-four.
His overturned convertible a fact, whitewall tires
like spinning plates, spliced with a spidery sound-
track, its own kind of action painting.
We're a species known to abuse drugs.
Curious how sightings of hovercraft
in lower-populated areas of the continent
underscore our innate need to pin loneliness
in place. Crop circles require an aerial view,
among birds only the bowerbird is artisan enough
to claim a critical eye. They decorate nests
for life, however long, the females wigged
and even-tempered, capable of final decisions.
So yeah, I promised to tape off the ceiling. And do,
picturing Lee Krasner and all those spent tubes.

Sound Navigation
and Ranging

Proof we worked to get here.
Amid freshwater-habitat complaints, hull creaks
speak for us, lake licking gunmetal.
Our presence like a shot of Irish
plummeting to the lager's glass bottom.
Success is forever, my friend,
outmanoeuvring our best attempts.
Less red meat. Vocab builders in the Lexus
on the freeway to the day job.
Retirement at sixty. Growing certain
we'll have no more to say once we've made it.
Our *summa cum laude* brains told us
to stretch resources, diversify, pressure our children
for grandchildren – as if migrating had a purpose
other than mere season.
In concert with interference patterns
in the currents, these lures we picked predawn
mimic in flash and wiggle
how many eons of process? We've put in our hours,
putted away mornings, pulled all-nighters,
fervent as Deadheads, humourless as Dagwoods,
cued to power in a Baconian age.
Francis One and Francis Two.
Woke up on occasion
with cocks cooling under strange sheets.
Not meaning to. Giving meaning the slip
through well-oiled hinges at the crime scene –
back to the boardroom, consultant's fees,

sushi on the corporate dime.
Sparkling, never tap.
Oftentimes went to dream and thrashed
as though throwing ourselves against padded walls.
Is it fair to say? on your behalf?
Not undone, but not unmoved
when shown forgiveness, mistaking it for love.
Recommitting to sameness and the weekend's fleece.
'A crying shame,' you'd declare
were you to lift your gaze from the surface tension
punctured by your line. You thumb
the trolling motor's remote to adjust our drift
towards the littoral weed bed, careless
with the up-to-thirty pounds of thrust
hunkered on the bow
like a curious house cat doubling its reflection.
Each volt twitch scares the fish we've come to catch
and toss back to murky lochness. From which:
Socrates. Tiktaalik. Trilobite. Eukaryote.
Beyond our ken, critical paths
swashbuckle to determine the one
we sense, catalogue, act upon.
Errol down the banister fends off villain after villain –
we're onshore, clothes clingy with mist
and gamy perspiration. Buckled up.
Trading the rare quip on the home slope.

Cast in Order
of Appearance

You're at a remove, off by
a positive integer of foam-firm seats: one
no less insurmountable for being the first.
Here I am. We are.
The north wall's second hand
shoos away our appointment with august airs.
What I could do with reindeer bone, knapped flint,
repeated lunar coincidence.
Scratch out intervals as timekeeper, or
be a hero! Reach up and swat the buttons,
switch from soap opera to news crawl.
The waiting room is at capacity, our hems and haws
swell into one beastly snuffle, perfect for
the opening crane shot of an ominous … whatsit …
okay, that shoe squeak might be psychogenic,
but its frequency is freaking me out.
Ah, *title sequence*. I finish the thought.
Consciousness makes the universe.
Empathy, the bubbles fissuring the spout.
Low pain thresholds add no more than a qubit
to the huddle our species adopts
by default: yes you, texting girl, stubborn
in your down. Old man already unbuttoned
at the waist, a wee morning oversight
and/or cry for help. Bowed as if
internal force could collapse a diagnosis.
Probability finds you, love, smeared,
your present condition unknown

beyond local symptoms we've all come to accept –
biological imperative, cause-effect –
which remakes the much-lobbed question, 'Who's next?'
as the blob, the thing, the shining.
It smothers us with normal,
though we cleave to standard deviations
under low-glare, polarized fluoresence.
Enter Nurse Ratchet (minus the starch) to read off
a name from her clipboard, no inflection,
ringing up another F on the Turing test.
The greybeard who's next, halving again each step,
races ellipses across the linoleum,
spoor dissipating under piped-in easy listenin'
and general winter flatulence.
His vacant seat is filled promptly
by another starstruck extra; they never fail
to hit their mark or glance away from the lens.
I'm near convinced by their nonchalance
they've got nothing to do with us.
Watch that plucky one book a follow-up.
A little shaky, perhaps? I send her off
with a prognosis worse than yours
because she is expendable and you are not.

Notes

The opening epigraph is from Mary Ruefle's poem 'Depicted on a Screen.'

'Paleosubwoofer': In the early nineties, Mattel issued a Barbie with 270 programmed phrases for the doll to speak. One of them, 'Math class is tough,' has entered the collective memory as 'Math is hard.'

'En Passant': The Nabokov quote comes from his story 'A Busy Man,' first published in 1931.

'That Stratospheric Streak My Green Filament' borrows phrases in sequence from two paragraphs on page 289 of *The End of Time: The Next Revolution in Physics* by Julian Barbour. As the title suggests, the book presents evidence for the nonexistence of time.

'Heads We Win, Tails You Lose': In *Jaws*, Robert Shaw improvised not the song but a monologue about the USS *Indianapolis*. By this time it is night, and Quint, Hooper and Chief Brody are at sea, alone on the boat. We all remember what happens next.

'Regular Folks Going Bananas': The lyric fragment is from the song 'If I Had a Hammer,' written by Pete Seeger and Lee Hays. Leonard Nimoy covered the song in 1968 for his album *The Way I Feel*.

'Size Extra Medium' owes a debt to a monthly catalogue for Hedonics, a company that specializes in Really Really Neat Stuff™.

'Nine Exes in a Silo, Pt. 1': The epigraph is from the song 'What Is Love?' It came out on Howard Jones's 1983 album *Human's Lib*.

'Primed for Contact': The male bowerbird decorates bowers, not nests.

Acknowledgements

Some of these poems appeared previously in the following journals and magazines: *Arc, The Puritan, The Fiddlehead, The Malahat Review, Taddle Creek, American Scientist, The Walrus, Hobo* and *Event*. My gratitude to the editors.

Much appreciation goes to the Canada Council for the Arts, the Ontario Arts Council and the Toronto Arts Council for their financial assistance.

Love to my wife, Charmaine, ace first reader and everything else besides.

Linda Besner and Steve McOrmond read the first draft of the manuscript and their comments were both generous and keen. Thanks, you two.

Jeramy Dodds saw these poems early, often and late. He made them better where they needed to be better and kept me from making them worse with a steadfast enthusiasm and a super-strong headlock. Thanks, Jer.

Cheers to the Coach House team, Alana Wilcox, Evan Munday and Leigh Nash, whose hard work and mad skills continually put me in a position to succeed.

Without Kevin Connolly, I'm not sure where I'd be as a writer – but I sure don't like thinking about it. Thanks, my friend, for the many rounds of unflinching edits and the many more years of encouragement.

About the Author

This is Matthew Tierney's third book of poetry. His second, *The Hayflick Limit*, was shortlisted for a Trillium Book Award and won the K. M. Hunter Award. He lives in Toronto.

Typeset in Aragon and Aragon Sans, from Canada Type.

Printed in July 2012 at the old Coach House on bpNichol Lane in Toronto, Ontario, on Zephyr Antique Laid paper, which was manufactured, acid-free, in Saint-Jérôme, Quebec, from second-growth forests. This book was printed with vegetable-based ink on a 1965 Heidelberg KORD offset litho press. Its pages were folded on a Baumfolder, gathered by hand, bound on a Sulby Auto-Minabinda and trimmed on a Polar single-knife cutter.

Edited by Kevin Connolly
Designed by Alana Wilcox
Author photo by Charmaine Tierney
Cover photograph, *Time Out*, by Julie Blackmon, courtesy of the artist

Coach House Books
80 bpNichol Lane
Toronto ON M5S 3J4
Canada

416 979 2217
800 367 6360

mail@chbooks.com
www.chbooks.com